NO

READ

LIMIT

.

Robert Hanshew

© Robert Hanshew, 2023
All rights reserved

Published in the United States of America
by Twist of Blue Poetry Publications

ISBN: 979-8-218-17402-6

Typset by Twist of Blue Poetry Publications

Cover Photograph and graphics by the author.

Acknowledgements

The author kindly thanks his two sons, Nathan and Damian. Besides his immediate family, whom he loves dearly, Robert also gives thanks to Susan Block Lynn Smith, Rachel Birchley, Mark Newbold, Marvin Barrish, Aldona Dyk, Dasha Ermeeva, and Leda Buzjak for their patience and critiques while I tested the material.

Contents

Don't Want Your Rewards 1

The Nearsighted Gunslinger 2

I Love You (But Just Don't Touch Me) 3

Doesn't Move Like Jagger 4

I Swear 5

The Librarian 6

Bad Troll 7

Half Full 8

Paparazzi 9

The Cure 10

Got No Emoji 11

Relationshipped 12

Lip-Glossed 13

Lost at IKEA 14

Can't Stay In My Lane 15

I Unmade My Bed (Now I Have to Lie In It) 16

The Finger 17

Braless 18

Ain't No Cowboy 19

Being Born 20

The Unlucky Knot 21

Don't Like Some Things 22

Chopping the Tree 23

The Last Meal 24

Diabolical 25

A Gesture 26

Hot Coffee 27

Mutation 28

If I Cook for You (Will You Still Love Me) 29

Don't Text Mommy 30

When Music Is X 31

Sordid, Torrid Affair 32

Combustfun 33

A Little Bird 34

Mistaken Medicine 35

Never Gonna Wake Me 36

Deal with the Devil 37

Stalled 38

You Could Take Those Off! 39

Glass House 40

The Overchiever 41

Don't Wanna 42

Dead Man's Blues 43

Impurrfect 44

Cookied 45

Sir, Do Not Put That There 46

Simply Horological 47

Turn Back Time 48

Badass 49

Old Rock Star Boyfriend 50

Tested	51
Neutered and Microchipped	52
Dafuq	53
Texting Is Not for Me	54
My Ghost Is An Asshole	55
Devil Joker	56
Opposites Attract	57
Forget I Forget	58
The Magician Stripper	59
F*** You, Mr. BMW	60
Just Can't Stay (When You Are Around)	61
Cracked Up	62
Scrooge on the Move	63
Sex as a Weapon	64
A Nudity Issue	65
Knock Em' Dead	66
When in Rome (People Do What I Do)	67
It's Now or Never	68
You Don't Want Me to Eat With You	69
Yogaed	70
Possessed	71
Can't Wait for the Day to End	72
When Karma Hit Amber	73
Do I Really Have To Clean?	74
Chocolate Croissant	75
Driving Jesus	76

A Little Prick	77
His Tail	78
Gooey-Bubbling Froth	79
Caught in Traffic	80
Be So Hip You Hop	81
Served	82
Black Bikini	83
Autocorrected	84
A New Swear Word	85
I Love You (But Not You)	86
Dead or Alive	87
You Really Gotta Hold On Me	88
How I Cam To Be	89
You Might Be Beautiful (If I Could Only See You)	90
Gift from Above	91
Risen to the Occasion	92
Funkytown	93
Leaf Blower	94
Good Fortune	95
Loser Boyfriend	96
The King and The Queen	97
In the Sand	98
Won't Grow A Mustache	99
Sister Mary Screwed	100
Exercising Demons	101
Island Man	102

Double-Triple Chocolate Cake	103
The Monk	104
Sleaze Hippies	105
X-Rayed	106
Better Be Annoying (Before Annoying Annoys You)	107
Art Class	108
Shrink, Shrank, Shrunk	109
Don't Care If I Ever Deliver	110
So What?	111
That Sinking Feeling	112
Don't Want to Fly Today	113
So What?	114
Where's the Check	115
A Hat Trick	116
Coffee and a Cigarette	117
First Impressions	118
Rock N' Roll Blues	119
When I Was Rowdy	120
Rock N' Roll Prescription	121
Fountain of Youth	122
Nothing Wrong with Cheating	123
Never Going to Catch me	124
Yet Another Way to Die	125
Handheld Device	126
Nothing is Beautiful Before 10:00 a.m.	127
Morally Condomed	128

Just Can't Suck Today	129
Frankly Dear, You Can Just Kiss It	130
Bandits	131
So Dirty	132
Don't Mess With Texting	133
She's Crazy for You	134
Don't Say I'm Beautiful – You Bastard	135
Opposites Don't Attract	136
Fingered	137
Dog Gone It	138
The Make-Up Artist	139
Adam Was Eve'd	140
Poison Ivy	141
Paranotnormal	142
Dracula Is My Mailman	143
The Influencer	144
Folk-Singer Son-In-Law	145
Nanasty	146
A Form of Expression	147
The Trash That Wouldn't Leave	148
Saw Mommy Stripping for Santa Claus	149
Unsubscribed	150

Don't Want Your Rewards

Don't want to be part of a rewards program
Nor do I want your boring spam
Frankly, I don't go shopping that often
So, don't tempt me with a half-off item

Not everything has to be tied together
A seller has now become a beggar
Tired of being asked at every store
If I want to come back once more

Not natural for me to be in any kind of mall
Over broken glass, well, I'd rather crawl
Don't need beautiful people looking beautiful
Really cannot use gadgets that are unusable

The cashiers always seem to be rather upset
For my loyalty card for that lower percent
Just can't bothered to remember to bring it
Too tired for even that kind of relationship

Only want to pay for items as marked
It's just the way I have been taught
Asked so many times, I may be in asylum
Yet, I only entered the store for one item

The Nearsighted Gunslinger

Was the fastest in the West
Defeated every bad-ass I met
Confused by my circle glasses
My foes always took chances

My hand was the quickest
Desperados always did tricks
Only ending up facing down
Guns back in holster; the only sound

My bullets occasionally stray
Sometimes due to my troubled aim
But it comes down to dirty lenses
Not to how I hold my weapons

My opponents grasp deep fears
My bullet nearer than it appears
Cool, steel eyes look into souls
Bursting any of their hopes

Glasses are off while taking a bath
Hearing shots firing at my back
Quickly turning to aim into the veranda
Only to realize I grabbed a banana

I Love You (But Just Don't Touch Me)

It's about that time of evening
You tell me that I'm so appealing
I love you, but just don't touch me
Just cannot stand your goatee

You may find all of this hard to hear
But please just do not come near
No need to look deeply into my eyes
You know how I need my own time

The birds and bees are so tired
They no longer have that desire
So, why don't you just fall asleep
At your age, it's all you need

It will be the same when we wake
Your face will look like a plague
You're still charming to be with
But just don't try to give me a kiss

Honey, you will not change my mind
So, please do not touch my behind
Those days of passion no longer exist
I'll just stop cooking if you persist

Doesn't Move Like Jagger

Music stars are not the same today
None seem to have any male rage
Take the current star on the chart
Could never match any rock star

One star tries dance routines on stage
Been years since he's been straight
Is forbidden to give any of his blood
But we are not allowed to judge

Tries to do splits and somersaults
But lifted back up by bodyguards
Doesn't move at all like Jagger
Only aching like a headmaster

Bengay will not help at all
Nor will any amount of alcohol
Perhaps a massage with icy hot
And a groupie will hit the spot

The band calls out for an encore
The star just cannot bend anymore
Bowing to enormous applause
Can't stand straight until his massage

I Swear

Getting through life has been easy
Only because I tend to swear freely
Came to me a such an early age
Have never known another page

People who know me -- understand
Those who don't -- want to reprimand
Don't really give a **** about them
Don't mind getting saucy once again

Authority, it doesn't like such a word
But once said, it cannot be unheard
Funny, how a judge doesn't like ****
Yet, he likes to do it to love

Some say I swear more than a sailor
But I am only doing normal behavior
In fact, who doesn't swear anymore?
It's fun; I only want to do it more

Occasionally, people do find it offensive
Eventually, they do come to their senses
And when an outburst of mine is done
Most people do not believe I am a Nun

The Librarian

Deviled horn rims
Make gangsters wince
Hell has never felt such fury
Like this literature bully

Don't get caught eating
In staff reserved seating
Doesn't mind wood on skin
The pleasure behind her grin

Before a book is overdue
She'll send a text just a bit rude
No poetry contained within
Only old-lady chagrin

Don't get caught talking
She loves her flogging
Leaving Dewey Decimal
Her scars so professional

For someone so surly
She won't become wordy
You'll only be put over her knee
Then punished with a dictionary

Bad Troll

Woke up on the bad side of the forest
Not really wanting to deal with a tourist
Just want to lie in the leaves and a dream
Been awhile since I floated upstream

Hear the tip-tap of a sweaty jogger
They are always a bit of a problem
Flicking my fingers just a little bit
A vine appears to make them trip

Really don't like weekend campers at all
Lighting fires and singing all night long
Wiggling my nose dark clouds begin to form
Honestly, they belong wet under a storm

Games are part of this unusual tradition
This fact should immediately raise suspicion
Have to hide because of a thrown lawn dart
A fast frisbee almost scalped me in the dark

When seen, humans call me a troll
Yet they are ones eating potato casserole
Venturing into nature to eat such things
Really, something is wrong with human beings

Half Full

Going to the bar full of glass and swank
Where the rude bartender wears his Arsenal mask
Always asking for a Guinness after a long hard day
But he seemingly doesn't understand whatever I say

When my Guinness arrives, it's always half empty
If I say something, his anger is then directed at me
He tells me instead that my Guinness is half full
In a manner, seemingly, always obnoxiously rude

It happens to be same situation time after time
If I state half empty; I'm the one who has crossed the line
His demeanor is other than worldly; he is just crass
Tired of him ignoring me, and his lack of class

Don't know what to do as the ladies are so beautiful
So, I have patience with my pint being half full
But, as life goes on, it just rubs me the wrong way
Paying for a half pint given to me day after day

Today, when the Guinness is delivered, it is half empty
Served with an attitude more than just less friendly
After, the bartender says my tip is less than usual
Accordingly, I tell him that my tip is only half-full

Paparazzi

Don't care about how you feel
Need to get a good shot on my reel
Gotta catch you with your mistress
Life is the constant wants next

Remember when stars had class
Not only Botox and pumped ass
Even marriage vows meant nothing
News stories were usually comforting

The power to do nothing but good
Is where news became misunderstood
Paparazzi began to show the bad
Onion peels behind the mask

Been to the dentist too many times
Been pushed through plenty of glass
Been threatened by mafia thugs
Been beat up by paid-off cops

Yet, that will not stop my plans
Gotta catch another girl in your hands
Will never stop as I am a paparazzi
Gotta get the dirt on a celebrity

The Cure

Harry was so tired of being bald
With it, all the names he was called
Sick of the finger points and laughs
Such as he is an old stripper's ass

Looking through the unclean fridge
Laid a cabbage bag he had missed
More than ripe, it really did stink
And the leaves were brown or pink

Rushing, he fell from the strong color
Ripping the bag, the contents went all over
Landing upon his huge cratered-bald spot
Suddenly, the area became incredibly hot

All around, his hair grew out like wildfire
Every hour, it raised just a bit higher
Seizing upon his new fantastic discovery
He became rich and trustworthy

Bald men grew hair in confidence
Every moment was simply marvelous
Oddly, they also began to speak Spanish
A strange side effect of the rotten cabbage

Got No Emoji

Received another text
Don't know what it meant
Just what is all this stuff
Please end, I've had enough

Hear yet another ping
Fingers can't do that swing
Just don't care to look
Even if I rather should

Just got no emoji
Need to win the lottery
Fingers can't be typing
While I do my fake smiling

Don't ask for a cut and paste
I'll only just make a mistake
My screen is also so dirty
I should not be so flirty

Just got no emoji
Texting is unholy
Don't want to phone
People just leave me alone

Relationshipped

Before I knew it, my wife changed
As with every marriage, it wasn't the same
Every situation had a different meaning
And, with that, a different reasoning

What once meant everything was okay
Suddenly, it became so risqué
Shouts became replaced by screams
Each day based on different themes

With this, my life became so very hard
Every day was dealt a new tarot card
Never believed in astrology or a horoscope
Shouldn't have never eloped

Plotting in the attic, I needed to escape
But, here, I felt safe behind the barricade
Never knew when I may say the wrong word
Or the perception of what she may have heard

After contemplation, I became very brave
Descending, I sweated while I prayed
We chatted, but my ad-libs turned it south
Now I watch YouTube in the dog house

Lip-Glossed

Could be the toughest guy around
But no match when she is in town
Tousled hair as if from the seventies
Invited to all the glamorous parties

Whenever she walks through the door
She is what men want but only more
Both lips bounce with deep shades of red
An image any man simply won't forget

Every man only comes to find heartache
Their burning desire a natural mistake
Hypnotized by undergarment crisscross
Transfixed by her soft, moist lip-gloss

Some men just fall backwards in coffins
Whenever she twists her hair so exotic
Cupid shooting unlimited supply of arrows
Ensuring men only feel endless woes

Nothing has changed since the dawn of time
Every poet searches for the perfect rhyme
Just to have her one day within their arms
While ignoring everything she harms

Lost at IKEA

My better half decided our day off
Without her, well, I just might lost
Telling me we are going to IKEA
Immediately, I dreaded her idea

Reverse parking our imported car
Ensuring we didn't have to walk far
Walking into the busy store lobby
Grabbing a shopping cart so wobbly

Quickly, it seemed as if we are in a maze
Confused by directions; lost in a haze
Thinking kitchen items are for the bath
Cell phone reception poor at the back

Looking at numbers for measurements
Not really sure what the numerals meant
Wishing the café served an alcoholic drink
Perhaps, this would help to make me think

At one point, I just want to hide then cry
Going back to check items time after time
Finally, making our way to the checkout
Only to be back at the front, I loudly shout

Can't Stay In My Lane

I'm the best driver around
Know every inch of this town
Can get out of any cop chase
My tires set the road ablaze

Rules are for those who follow
Live or die is the simple motto
Other drivers are only in my way
No tomorrow; only today

Just can't stay in my lane
Something I cannot change
Speed is my illusive mistress
Not constrained by law's limits

The judge says I will meet my maker
Nothing is in my money shaker
God will always let me pass
Though I drink during mass

Universe is ruled by utter chaos
Just like my dirty windshield wipers
Speeding to death's destination
To that light in the sky – my damnation

I Unmade My Bed
(Now I Have to Lie In It)

Making my bed was never a high priority
Tight corners were always a formality
A properly made bed is like a coffin
Can only relax when the sheets soften

Haven't made my bed now in years
Stale cookies have become souvenirs
When ladies come to spend the night
I have something for my appetite

Perhaps, I should buy another set
But, the designs I have are perfect
Nothing beats a tropical forest design
As one doesn't notice the spilled wine

My mother would sign-the-cross
If she could see the dried sauce
Not caring about the exact stain
But the bed looks like a hurricane

Should I change this evil way?
Well, it will not happen today
Chinese take away coming soon
And somewhere here is my lost spoon

The Finger

Weddings are nothing but obnoxious
Two in love make me simply nauseous
For most, it is simply nothing but a game
Cupid has never had really good aim

Sitting at a relative's summer wedding
The groom looks as if at a beheading
My uncle must be holding a rifle
Or so it was said upon my arrival

She looked sick walking down the aisle
To be fair, the groom also looks just as vile
At this point, feet kicked my wicker chair
Turning around, no one seemed to be there

Sadly, my wife's family were also invited
Their emotions are always just unexcited
Again, knocks begin moving my seat
All to the rhythm of an annoying beat

Had to be the boy whose nose was runny
His jokes during vows were so unfunny
Turning to give the finger as the last straw
Only to find out it was my mother-in-law

Braless

My breasts are splendid
Going as nature intended
Representing today's state
Perky and upright without tape

Hearing only yells and whistles
Open-armed hugs and blown kisses
Should have done this years ago
Every day needs a little side-show

Older ladies seem a bit upset
They miss a come-on and a cigarette
They miss that midnight game
Which left a little nicotine stain

Husbands are afraid to look
Easy fish to land on a hook
Nothing better than them getting hit
No matter how quick their wit

Hearing nothing now but shouts
Even from women in the crowds
Only stares and glares at the mall
So, why should I put my bra back on?

Ain't No Cowboy

Won't find me riding a horse
Nor will I call you sir
Will never be a cowboy
My pants are corduroy

Stetson Hats are never cool
Only looks good on a mule
Don't try to put one on me
Not even for a selfie

Won't find me with a lasso
Nor speaking ever so slow
Will never be a cowboy
My milk will always be soy

Denim pants are too tight
For my manhood's copyright
They need to breathe
Not tied up on a leash

Won't find me with boots
Nor with tobacco juice
Never will wear spurs
Only fashionable fake furs

Being Born

Relaxing in the only world I know
Soon, this world I will soon outgrow
My legs cannot stretch as they used to
Honestly, I think I am severely overdue

Don't want to face the stupid world
Don't' want to face life so absurd
Perhaps, I can just stay a bit longer
Really don't want to meet my father

Suddenly, it all seems a bit wrong
Can't be soothed by a nursery song
Seems that my mother wants me out
She is tired of me being a lay-about

Hearing the voice of that one doctor
His poking is nothing but torture
When I am older, I will get revenge
His perversion assures him to be French

My mother begins to violently scream
It must be part of their scheme
Born, the crazy doctor highly lifts me
Smirking, I aim and begin to pee

The Unlucky Knot

Bad luck runs in Lucy's family
But she lives her life happily
Despite having only bad luck
Her quacks are happy, like a duck

She really does have a good life
Her come backs are always wise
She also has a very crude tongue
Always used with a clever pun

She was chosen to give a speech
On the benefits of smoking weed
It helps to lower blood pressure
Though it makes the eyes redder

Her speech dress was old but sexy
Yet she was unkempt and messy
Lucy turned the heads of all the men
With her style of a hot-mess meme

Toking, she stepped on stage
Tripped on ropes not tied straight
Falling, she tore her elegant dress
Then said, " I'm still *your* Royal Highness"

Don't Like Some Things

Some say I have a sweet tooth
Just don't some things; I'm not rude
Vegetables are fruits from the devil
To eat beans, for that, I will not settle

Can't eat seafood from my auntie
I'd rather eat cupcakes in the alley
One should never eat crustaceans
Not even in the most trying situations

Always carry a cookie bag or two
Never know when they maybe only stew
Can't stand soups, so smelly and gooey
Rather have a doughnut so chewy

Wasn't born this way to be honest
Got tired of all those special sauces
Eating spongey animals is not normal
After eating, I just want to gargle

Please serve me what I would like
Seriously, do I have to ask all the time?
Just give me a big dessert menu
Treat me, please do not be cruel

Chopping the Tree

Being a perfectionist is a problem
You see, a tree outside doesn't blossom
Been slowly dying for a couple of years
Everything has to have a good appearance

Michael decided to chop down the tree
Didn't realize there would be that much debris
In the back of his mind, it would be a problem
So, he placed the pieces in an organized column

The landscaping crew kept on ignoring his calls
Not a good sign, something is bound to go wrong
Other offices began to ask questions everyday
Being shy, he never knew really what to say

Michael began to leave out from the back
His answer to the local song and dance
Before long, he grew to be rather hopeless
This trait was also part of his usual neurosis

On a dark, rainy day, he heard a hard knock
The authorities explained, it was quite a shock
The chopped tree was literally one in a million
Planted by none other than Abraham Lincoln

The Last Meal

Twas the night before the criminal's death
He didn't do it; but he stupidly confessed
The biased jury found him guilty nonetheless
As with anything in life, he has no regrets

Today, he would have his last meal
No court wanted to hear his appeal
The chief would prepare anything he wanted
He asked for chocolates and a huge sausage

The warden stared at him for a few minutes
Well, the convict didn't need anything nutritious
Before long, he was called out for his last meal
In his back pocket, he had poison concealed

Eating the huge sausage, he had a big smile
While the police were busy, he opened the vile
Quickly, spreading it on the chocolates
Giving them away, the guards became nauseous

Before long, they were gasping for their lives
As the grew silent, the convict got into a disguise
Walking for days, he searched around in his pocket
Hungry, he mistakenly, ate a piece of that chocolate

Diabolical

Rules are for those petty in life
Also, for laws, I just do not have time
My finger is shown to such authority
Jailing all those of us who are free

My soul cannot be captured by law
Modern life, well, I wish I could uninstall
The plug on conformity must be pulled
Tired of these man-made imposed rules

Both God and the Devil want to talk
My attitude scares both of their flock
Seems that my lack of caring for either
Made me special, though, I want neither

Tempting me with angels and lust
Funny that both in me have such trust
Don't need them to help me being saved
Their literature, sadly, I have misplaced

Since birth, I have been called diabolical
By never wanting either Heaven or Hell
Who really cares about life after Death?
For both of them, your soul is forever in debt

A Gesture

Come from the wrong side of the tracks
Where people are dressed in dirty rags
She comes from a small European country
Where people always seem to have money

Somehow, we had that romantic spark
Fell in love just over some small talk
She loved how I slowly poured my gravy
I just loved that I had a date daily

Wanted to give her a present with love
But, for presents, I never had enough
Couldn't give her a typical romantic gift
It had to be worthy of big, deep kiss

Went to her Embassy to ask questions
The staff member had good suggestions
We looked through an old cultural book
Until I found one that had me hooked

Little did I know he was her old boyfriend
He was looking to only have some revenge
The evening only ended up with hurtful cries
As the present meant I hope her dog dies

Hot Coffee

Hot coffee is a commodity
Preparation is a true calling
A barista who can create
Is something to celebrate

Independent or chain cafes
There are always delays
Machines or employees broken
Lattes cold or almost frozen

All I want or need
Is simply a hot coffee
Why is it so hard?
It's such an easy mark

No need to even try tea
Simply, it is not for me
Nothing is cool about tea bags
Kept on dirty dish rags

All I want – is something hot
Don't want it if it's not
Barista, just heat the water up
And quickly pour it in my cup

Mutation

Metal hair growing down to the arse
Middle fingers pointed at the boss
Playing air guitar at conference calls
Singing about whom has the biggest balls

The CEO has become outraged and upset
The metal head is quickly putting him in debt
The head banger could simply be rewired
But, sadly, he does know law and can't be fired

Corporate meetings held day and night
Must be gotten rid off, but not with crime
They decide to do a little bit of voodoo
His personality will change with work juju

Putting some magical witch dust in his soda
Suddenly, he has the urge to do some yoga
His sarcastic sayings are slowly going away
Even asking how people are doing today

Showing up next with a haircut and shave
Along with a dull suit that is business safe
The magic has worked, pure subtle mutation
A perfect worker; part of the corporation

If I Cook for You (Will You Still Love Me)

Know how to make you fall in love
The way to your heart is with some grub
Let me grill my good, juicy steak
Served with vegetables on the plate

Expertly taught how to steam a beet
A simple, lovely red — just so sweet
Served with a vegetarian chicken breast
So fresh, as if brought in from the nest

If I cook for you, will you love me?
Would you call me for every evening tea?
Let me show how much I really care
My prepared meals hold such debonair

My dressing will sprinkle on your salad
Delicate with toss, never ever splashed
Layered with sliced tomatoes and onions
Dashed, with those crunchy soft croutons

My desserts will leave you wanting more
Custard surprises; never know what's in store
My coffee brews instant air intoxication
Divine cocoa, cream; such a revelation

Don't Text Mommy

Mommy needs a day off
Can't hide anymore in the garage
My turn to take care of the kids
Giving her a comforting kiss

Now, kids don't text mommy
If you do, it will be very naughty
Remember the last time you texted
I had to move into the local bedsit

If things get destroyed, it's okay
Remember mommy is away
We can easily get a replacement
A lot of extras are in the basement

Doesn't matter if you play inside
Won't be the first time we lied
Just don't break her new vase
If you do, things will not be the same

Now, let me catch up on football
Oh No! I hear a crash down the hall
The kids are playing like a tsunami
But, now kids, just don't text mommy

When Music Is X

Everything has become limp
It seems I have lost an inch
Just can't cut the mustard
My muscles once were hard

Impossible to lift anything
Too hard to pull a string
Perhaps, I can't be bothered
No magic works I've conjured

Should I care, should I really?
But even my chest hair is filthy
May have to take some vitamins
But is truth tied to any science?

Music might just be my answer
Rock, Pop, Disco, does it matter?
Any beat shakes my walls
My arse dances to any song

Suddenly, my muscles flex
Energy is again in my step
Dancing out my front door
My spirit is too hard to ignore

Sordid, Torrid Affair

No-one needs love
Only ever need it once
But when she walked in
My lust just had to begin

Some say, it was a mistake
To date someone her age
Love keeps one so young
Yet she could be my mom

She takes care of all my needs
Keeps an extra set of keys
Knows my favorite shops
Ensuring our love never stops

Some say she is using me
But my love is hers for free
Our love keeps her young
Treating me as if I am her son

Now, men do this all the time
And, for them, it isn't a crime
Don't mind about her missing teeth
Her kisses are all I have dreamed

Combustfun

A follower of fashion
Not knowing any passion
Simon wanted to belong
But his will was not strong

Very nearsighted since birth
With age, it only became worse
Didn't know the metric system
Nor did he understand fission

Didn't matter to him anymore
Normal life was just a bore
He wanted to make an impact
Explosions were his modern jazz

Working all day and night
He bravely slept upright
No one would be harmed
Tomorrow at the local college

The day had quietly arrived
Igniting the button on time
Upon the clearing of smoke
The audience were without clothes

A Little Bird

Jayne was the movie star of her age
A bright light amongst the decay
She caught the eye of an actor
Dapper, but not really a dancer

With his shaken and stirred martini
Gary thought he looked so dreamy
Could have been a Three Stooge
But, in true reality, is more of a boob

He said, "A little bird told me you like me."
She looked at him as if he was a nobody
"Run your fingers through my hair," he stated
She sat silent while he patiently waited

Gary said," Let us make something happen."
Shrugging, she didn't know what he was asking
"Come on, let's go for a romantic walk," he asked
Jayne just could not be bothered by this ass

Reaching around, Gary decided to hug
Making her squirm with ancient sea-faring musk
Jayne said, "A little bird can only really tell lies
And, by your hug, you are too small of a size"

Mistaken Medicine

Nothing worse than a bad day at work
Dealing with people who just smirk
Driving back home wasn't any better
Dodging cars in somewhat icy weather

Living with a pharmacist surely has perks
But his aspirin has only made me feel worse
The bedroom walls seem to be closing in
From there, I don't know where to begin

Everywhere I look, the world is wiggling
The paintings on the wall are giggling
The sky turns from midnight to daylight
A second seems like a long hour of time

The stairs seem to be over a mile long
Stepping, nothing seems to be wrong
Descending, the front door quickly opens
The world outside stands still in a moment

Slowly walking around Mr. and Mrs. Jones
Each holding their outdated cells phones
These funny side effects eventually do wear off
And I come to find myself naked on the lawn

Never Gonna Wake Me

Buzz, Buzz, Buzz
Tired of this alarm stuff
Never gonna wake me up
Give the noise some shove

No problem lying in
Not against any religion
Dreaming is in my bible
Snuggling isn't being idle

Work, Work, Work
Tired of that boss jerk
Just might go berserk
Wish I had a little dirt

Making money is for sheep
I'd rather lie in and sleep
Only avoiding temptation
No mood for damnation

Buzz, Buzz, Buzz
Why all this fuss?
Never gonna wake me up
Gonna hit snooze as I nudge

Deal with the Devil

The devil always visits my local café
Started to chat with him one particular day
He seemed what some might say naïve
Everything I said he somehow did believe

Oddly, his favorite drink was an iced latte
Didn't matter whatever the time of day
He never spoke about his wars or hate
The best coffee was our only debate

One day, decided to trick the devil
Couldn't help it; I just had to meddle
Asked him if he could turn up the heat
He didn't realize the intent of my misdeed

He relayed that people have had it too nice
After tortures, he would work on it that night
As I tossed and turned, my AC didn't help
My silk sheets seemed as if they were to melt

At the café, ladies were taking off clothes
So hot, didn't really care what was exposed
The devil entered and slowly looked around
Pranked, he turned to me then smiled

Stalled

When one has to go
Everything moves so slow
When all stalls are occupied
A second is an hour of time

Rushing into a local café
Ignoring what directions say
All the doors are locked
No one answers after I knock

Running to the local market
Cutting through the parking lot
Only to find the store is closed
Gotta find a stall or it will be gross

Thinking about the local library
That bathroom near Brazilian poetry
This area is filled with the homeless
And, my bladder, is utterly hopeless

Driving to the local mall
There has to be one stall
Just as soon as I close the door
I do not have to go anymore

You Could Take Those Off!

No need to wear those anymore
They belong locked in a drawer
A smile should be always shown
Not a covering over a mouth or nose

Tear them off your face
We are all not the same
Show the beauty within
The colors of your skin

Break the bond of obedience
Don't feel as if a deviant
Walk around and feel proud
Not stuck in society's slouch

Burn as if a lost memory
Take back that energy
Think of it as history
Not what one does daily

No need to wear those anymore
Life is worth something more
One shouldn't be constrained
We don't have to look the same

Glass House

Edgar's creativity endlessly twirled
Consulted the best architects in the world
Desired the best house on the street
Built with glass, not with concrete

Peter, an Avant-guard architect, had an idea
A glass house, but living without fear
The house would be made entirely of glass
Cost was no option as Edgar had the cash

Construction crews worked day and night
Handsomely paid for their blue-collar time
Before long, the house was completed
Cheering, the hard-working men succeeded

On paper, one could see out but not see inside
The glazing was installed but not truly tried
Edgar thought he could walk around nude
But everyone could see him in the bathroom

Taking the crowd outside as fan worship
They only wanted to see his legendary turnip
Then one day, a letter left him totally baffled
Informing him everyone could see his tackle

The Overchiever

Work was all dandy and fine
Now, it's on a continual decline
Our boss has become cheaper
All because of the overachiever

Hired just the other month
Now I daily eat a bottle of tums
Always has the quickest answer
But is only a corporate cancer

We just have to get rid of him
Reached the point of sink or swim
Should we destroy his thumbnail
Or send midget porn via his email

Just can't handle work and stress
Our desks should return to their mess
Tired of the hard, daily competition
Dreaming of our half-day intermission

Calling in for a meeting one morning
Fearful, as management is so boring
Smiling, telling us to meet the new boss
To our dismay, in the overachiever walks

Don't Wanna

Enjoying my tea too much
So please do not touch
I'm just not in the mood
Don't mean to be rude

Just don't want to make love
You may think it's just nuts
Don't need any of your hugs
Being with you just sucks

Really enjoy my free time
You don't have to be mine
Please don't try to be sexy
Shaking your boob belly

Just don't want to make love
I'd rather ride the bus
Please do not get nude
Honestly, I'm eating my food

Having fun being alone
Better being on one's own
Could try later on tonight
Who knows? I just might

Dead Man's Blues

Being dead cannot stop me
From attending a glorious party
Was invited before I apparently died
Told them I would attend when I replied

Don't like to let my friends down
At parties, I am always the clown
But, with my dead limp and white skin
Perhaps, as I appear, I won't be let in

The bouncer didn't seem to mind all
Though at any moment I could fall
The ladies didn't want to talk
Perhaps, it was my deathly cough

People stared as I drank the punch
Then, I heard a disheartening thud
My left leg feel off from my body
Sadly, it frightened everybody

Now, I didn't want to die
It wasn't the best of time
Shouldn't have had that forbidden kiss
As it put me on the mafia's dead list

Impurrfect

Noise breaks silence
Rubbing of the hands
Rising of the mist
Invisibility of wind

Everybody is gone
Silence is the alarm
Hiding under the sheets
Fangs giving me the creeps

The creaking of doors
Darkness of horrors
No noise is ever good
From knocks on wood

Someone walks around
Items fall to the ground
Silence echoes every sound
The wind blowing so loud

Noises on the steps
A ghost never forgets
The door slowly opens
My cat walks in with silence

Cookied

That time of year again
When cookie sales begin
School kids acting like sharks
Hoping for anyone to buy a box

Most people enjoy them
Think they are a slice of Heaven
To me, they are simply tasteless
Not sure if those are even raisins

Avoiding them is now a game
Can't say how they really taste
They will just stomp on my feet
So, I avoid them on any street

Can't answer when they knock
Looks like they will never stop
I'll hide for a bit in the bathroom
Soon, it will be their curfew

Now quiet, I open up the door
They are waiting by the store
Making me buy some after a bit
Good thing my cash is counterfeit

Sir, Do Not Put That There

People daily ignore any kind of rule
Usually, because, one is a stooge
Like a guy who puts a cold drink on a table
A behavior just so socially unstable

Doesn't think about the stains left behind
All the questions are just asking why
His world is in the court of oblivious
In fact, nothing in the world is serious

Approaching him over a minute or two
Seemingly knowing he would hear the truth
His eyes turned as I told him about his glass
Soon, his smirk turned into a laugh

Persistent, I scolded him about the stain
The destruction of a wood's beautiful grain
After a while, he contemplated and smiled
Informing me my info was simply worthwhile

Confident my message reached the man
And that my words were not only verbal spam
As I turned, I heard once again his gentle laugh
Then saw upon the table, that sweaty glass

Simply Horological

Horror night finally arrived
Ghosts stealing their usual time
Again, with my fiancée's parents
Only always end up just staring

Never have asked what I do
I find that behavior kind of rude
But they do have bazillion dollars
And I am tired living off carnivals

Arriving at the usual clock strike
Wearing my pink tie, they don't like
My fiancée looks simply dashing
No other way, I could ever imagine

Being served the dinner pudding
Questioning our jobs with foreboding
My fiancée's father says he's in Horology
Didn't quite understand what he told me

Asking about the techniques of his job
Must have said something completely wrong
He asks me how I came to that conclusion
As his job doesn't deal with prostitution

Turn Back Time

Listening to a snore and a fart
Just when did our love fall apart
Used to be like one in the beginning
But we have reached the last inning

If only I could turn back time
Perhaps I would be more wise
My man would be nice and kind
Not defined by acts so swine

Decisions based on a size and a ruler
Shouldn't be used for the future
Size of the heart is what matters
Not about those BMW factors

Caught onto the mystical
Transformed my physical
Found us when we were young
Dripped in honey with tongue

Refused his cheap words
Wrapped in shallow furs
Enjoying my sleep now in peace
Without that swine in my sheets

Badass

Can break stone with my bare hands
My thrust is stronger than any ax
Animals sense I shouldn't be messed with
They hear the thunder under my kilt

My colors paint over doom and gloom
With any type of sickness, I'm immune
Yes, folks, I am really that badass
My manhood is stronger than brass

My mother rocked the garden of Eden
My father was cast out of hell for treason
As a child, I created flame and fire
Then I stole an angel's wanton desire

Can withstand any type of bullet shot
Feathers in flight are simply caught
Lashes simply will never mark my skin
Will never feel a scorpion sting

Even the devil doesn't want to dance
He has seen the scars on my hands
I have the biggest ever set of balls
When I walk, they clack songs

Old Rock Star Boyfriend

Is this tossed scarf his or mine?
We tend to wear the same design
Not easy dating an old rock star
Always propped up at the local bar

The fans don't mind he not young
His tight pants still show he is well hung
Gyrating to the drummer's strong beat
The girls always seem to be in heat

Every day, drinking bottles of Jack Daniels
Takes him away from all the scandals
Like the affairs with political wives
Or the lawyers from former brides

Isn't as strong now to pick up a TV
Tends to reuse an old song for a new melody
Falls asleep at some of his rehearsals
But still extremely rich from commercials

Don't think he ever sees daylight
His pet cat is called snakebite
Wakes me up with guitar feedback
Only to see his plumber's crack

Tested

Studying for a final exam
All to get that diploma sham
Drank to remember answers
Asleep after a few chapters

Woke up long after my alarm
Rushing out feeling embalmed
Looking out for Building 101
How could I have been so dumb?

Rushing late into the room
Sitting down I felt such doom
Felt I was in a daydream
Each girl was out of a magazine

Couldn't concentrate on the test
Only on which breast was best
Every time I thought on a question
I only saw a beautiful freshman

Before long, I heard, "Test over."
Wishing I would have stayed sober
Thinking about what I was going to do
Only then seeing I was in Building 102

Neutered and Microchipped

Lying on crushed purple velvet
Brushing myself after another haircut
Staring at the loose fan on the ceiling
Thinking of lost sex and dreaming

Remembered when I fed their heat
Coming after me as I walked the street
My flowing mane just so luxurious
Now, when I walk, I feel hernias

Nothing but cramps in my stomach
My legs hurt and so do my buttocks
Now if I even think about having sex
My neck is sore; can't walk on my legs

These affairs went on year after year
Now, if they come, all I do is sneer
Just do not feel in the mood anymore
Only want to lie on my back and snore

Lying on my back, waiting for catnip
Something feels not unlike a metal chip
Just what has happened to poor ol' me
My fangs were all felines ever dreamed

Dafuq

Herman wanted a different sermon
The urge to do something uncertain
He was in the Navy back in the day
Seemed like he was always away

After a few coffees late at night
He was still having a difficult time
All his stories involved drink and sex
Nothing else was better to confess

He thought of those wanton times
Today, most of them would be crimes
The tale of him and that young lady
Still can't believe that was my baby

As the people arrived for mass
He shook hands and gave thanks
The mass went accordingly to plan
Then, the weekly sermon began

Lecturing about orgies and drink
The people didn't know what to think
Continuing, things began to run amok
Sitting, they only thought – What Dafuq?

Texting Is Not for Me

Woke up this morning rather beguiled
Thought I would be wearing my smile
Looked at my texts from last night
My stomach belched with fright

The emoji, to my love, made me a creep
She was offended I sent her a peach
So, I lovingly send her now a peace sign
Now, she texts I have such a dirty mind

Send her a hot dog to suggest dinner
She furiously calls me to bicker
Should have sent a letter to her mailbox
But no one bothers anymore with Microsoft

Repulsed by a banana and a doughnut
Only meant to meet at the coffee shop
Thinking of what to send her next
Nervous, I send her emoji sweat

My phone is hot and now blowing up
Must calm her as she is out for blood
Sending a popping champagne bottle
But it also means something awful

My Ghost Is An Asshole

Swear I just felt a strong poke
No-one around must be my ghost
Some have a guardian angel
My ghost is straight outta hell

Takes pride in ruining my everyday
As if a mother-in-law on extended stay
Ruins when my friends are over
As it burns food in the toaster

Never has liked any of my girlfriends
Turning my room to smell of rotten eggs
Honestly, my ghost is an asshole
Just a huge supernatural cat fur-ball

Likes to turn off the TV when I watch
Cruelly, always misplaces one of my socks
Some days I cannot find the set of keys
Only finding them in my Mac and Cheese

The church emailed they cannot perform miracles
The mafia texted they cannot change criminals
The police said they don't investigate an aberration
So, as I sit without TP, I live in damnation

Devil Joker

There are rumors about religion
Especially about the one they call Satan
He wasn't cast as we were taught
But due to his practical jokes on God

He was the first to use Whoopi cushions
Didn't mix well with the beautiful hymns
The angels would begin to giggle and laugh
This trick was offensive to God during mass

His red satin jackets were a distraction
Seriously, velvet isn't wanted in Heaven
The angels grew more and more upset
By the fake doggie doo on a cloud carpet

No-one liked his exploding-can surprise
Younger angels get wind in their eyes
God met with his others in his board room
How could they get him to change his tune?

One day, he asked God to smell a flower
Leaning in, the water came out in a shower
Not able to take any more, God began to yell
Despite pleas, the Devil was cast down to hell

Opposites Attract

Falling in love doesn't happen everyday
It's like winning a free holiday
Fell in love with a religious purist
I'm a rocker; she's a church organist

Somehow, we connected on the train
My nose rings didn't meet any disdain
Her clothes were simply out of fashion
But, somehow, there was an attraction

Her hairspray completely turned me on
Though on our first date we had a chaperon
On our next date we couldn't help ourselves
Making love as others recited prayers

My tattoos of devils didn't upset her
She made me dress up like a Monseigneur
Actually, my lover was simply a wild one
Though she dressed up as if she were a nun

All of my friends don't know what to say
Because at a concert she tends `to pray
Don't know how long this love with last
But they do say that opposites attract

Forget I Forget

Waking up these days is so hard
Everything has become is so wrong
Forgetting what I am supposed to do
Or why I even have stepped into the room

Some days, when stepping on the elevator
I remember my pants left on the refrigerator
My car keys are lost more than they are found
Using escalators, I go up instead of down

Have reached that stage of life where I forget
Instantly can't remember where I just stepped
They say this problem comes with a certain age
Prefer to think this situation is only just a stage

Do not know what I am really thinking now
Should I go shopping and get something in town
I am sure there is a product that I truly need
But, in the end, I could only be living in a dream

It's a miracle I am able to remember anything
Or what I am doing or where I have just been
To be honest, I do not know what will come next
Even right now, I'm just about to forget to forget

The Magician Stripper

Clothes have no meaning if worn
They should be ripped and torn
All I have to do is my exotic strip
Expertly placing my hands on my hip

On stage, I do my little dance
Suddenly, men are in a trance
My audience stands in awe
Bare midriff, my charm

My shoes slowly come off first
Then I sexily play with my shirt
Flashing a thigh or some boobs
Mesmerizing all the young dudes

Throwing my shirt into the audience
Trashy but yet not so obvious
Undoing my bra at certain points
Turning men instantly into boys

Topless, I go for my crimson panties
As tasteful as strawberry candies
Totally nude, all of them cheer
Lifting a curtain, I then disappear

F*** You, Mr. BMW

A BMW driver is miserable lothario
Should never sped with a loud radio
Yet, there always has to be one
A true to life faulty condom

Weaving in and out of my lane
Seems he is just playing a game
Doesn't care if he causes an accident
He'll just play off the ambulance

So, F*** You, Mr. BMW
We will again rendezvous
Don't know when or where
But, you and your care beware

Once again in my rearview mirror
Quickly, he easily becomes near
Blowing his horn at a stop sign
No patience, that utter swine

Passing me at the first chance
Just being the usual first-class ass
Behind him at the next red light
Now green, blowing my horn in delight

Just Can't Stay (When You Are Around)

Squared Tables and Round Glasses
You're so sour, lemons not apples
Remarks about this or whatever
Left or right, just never center

Just Can't Stay
When you are Around
Upon entering the room
I Could Just do Without

Polished silver and folded napkins
You're so vain, tactics, not answers
Talking about whom you don't like
Never a good word, only a dislike

Just Can't Stay
When you are Around
As soon as you enter
I feel a certain gesture

Dried flowers and candle wax
You're so bitter, classical not jazz
Wishing bad luck on whomever
Always an answer but never clever

Cracked Up

The day rose with a cluck
Already I have had enough
Trapped within circular white
Cannot escape by any side

Each day is new adventure
Life burning a splendor
Creative, spinning on an axis
Horizontal before trances

The day sings another crow
As the Sun settles for indigo
Rolling around on the floor
As if a wave upon your shore

Each night rises from ashes
Burnt from soul candles
Smoke rising like whispers
Carried by invisible fingers

The day continues as it does
The death of the rising Sun
Suddenly, I hear a hard smack
Onto the pan I slide as I crack

Scrooge on the Move

Finding youth so upsetting
Just where are we heading?
They don't make any sense
Please, look how they dress

My skull cane dazzles them
I've been on many a meme
They love it when I'm rude
And show my naughty tattoo

Even have a fan club
Selling t-shirts and stuff
Just a scrooge on the move
My crust defines being crude

Shaking my fists in rhythm
Everyone belongs in prison
Don't ever cross my path
Karens even fear my wrath

Never, ever, talk to me
You're just a young wannabe
Now, just don't treat me crass
If so, my cane will go up your ass

Sex as a Weapon

Harry didn't need sex anymore
Thought of it only as a man's chore
Wasn't an Old nor New Romantic
Pants didn't have belts but elastic

His wife, Patti, was at her bitter end
Didn't need sex but liked to spend
Harry simply paid to keep her away
A good arrangement that didn't change

One day, she needed a good romp
Cleaning naked with a mop
Entering the kitchen with a sway
But Harry only looked the other way

Patti wasn't easily one to give up
Any man will eventually give into lust
She only had to show a touch of boob
And Harry will slowly lose his cool

Calling to him later from the bath
A chance worthy of the math
Asking him, "Harry, let's make love"
Responding, it was his time of the month

A Nudity Issue

Remember when I could freely walk around
Feeling the sexy with my youthful bounce
Could stand in-front of any door or window
Women seemed pleased with my innuendo

These days I still walk around fully naked
And I love the way my boy is shaking
But people stop walking their dog and stare
When, and how, did life become so unfair?

Being young is clearly something to cherish
It's the period before one realizes ethics
Court cases are for the older generation
While young, nudity doesn't have any connotation

Now, the other day I received a rude letter
Upon reading it, I thought it was in error
My neighbors are upset I am walking nude
My behavior was what they call being rude

The community wants me to close my curtains
That is something I will never do; I am certain
They say my nude influence sets bad morals
But why should I hide my tasty morsels

Knock Em' Dead

People screaming no matter where I turn
Forgotten what I have learned
Just what does a stop sign mean again?
Knew I should have sent my identical twin

Life always seems to end up the same
The devil's poker playing that ol' game
Don't care about the beeping horns
Or if a car has scratched my doors

At a three-way red light that is out
Don't care about others so I shout
Always surprised people still use a finger
Should have expected that from a ginger

Just my luck there is a school bus ahead
Should I stop or should I just go instead
Again, I hear a bunch of screams and shouts
What foul language used by Boy Scouts

As I come to a stop at the driving center
The tester suddenly loses his temper
Son, you have failed your f****g test
Well, sir, but you *did* say to Knock Em' Dead

When in Rome (People Do What I Do)

Rome has become my second home
When there, I'm never am alone
Seems like I am high-paid model
Would Ignore me if I were normal

Am bit of a minor celebrity
All love my American obscenity
Like my zipper was down all day
Becoming a widely read fashion essay

When in Rome People do what I do
Nothing I do ever seems to be taboo
Let me wear my curtains as a sexy robe
Will then star at the next fashion show

My hygiene has decreased with fame
Fashion houses have made it a campaign
Soiled pants were on the catwalks
Also on show were my mismatched socks

Elegantly wasted in a historic park
Suddenly, it was fashionable after dark
Makes me wonder what will I do next?
Perhaps be nude with a tie of red velvet

It's Now or Never

So sweaty now the concert's over
Just may soon lose my composure
Need a peanut butter and banana sandwich
But somehow my obsession has vanished

Honestly, don't know what I will now do
All the *hangers-on* must leave the room
Dreaming of a big sandwich so thick
Then washing it down with some cold milk

Ask my driver to take me to the grocer
That, or any 7/11, don't care which is closer
Need some peanut butter for my bananas
Just cannot go back to eat a salad

Rushing through the store aisles
Ignoring all the disarrayed boxes in piles
My heart is pounding; it's now or never
A sign says "sold out"; must be an error

Store after store, both are sold out
My road crew searches all over town
My thoughts are racing; life is so unkind
With this sandwich always on my mind

You Don't Want Me to Eat With You

Aiming my potatoes at the ceiling
Gravy dripping, just so endearing
Just can't act my age while eating out
Must do what is not allowed

Reaching over others who are trying to eat
Trying to steal that good piece of meat
Don't really care what other people think
All food is game within my arm's reach

Carelessly pushing fruit around in my mouth
Making those seated around me have doubt
Perhaps, they should find another area to sit
As I just won't stop behaving like a little tit

Throwing biscuits into the air as if a ball
Biting into one if it happens to fall
People are turning chairs around out of spite
My behavior is wrong, but it feels so right

Taking more mashed potatoes than one can eat
Wondering if they would feel good on my feet
Taking all the desserts on the decorated tray
Should really behave better on my wedding day

Yogaed

Feeling a bit out of shape
Stomach looking like a grape
Learning a bit about yoga
Would rather be on the sofa

Began with a Mountain Pose
Not too hard I suppose
Tried the Downward Facing Dog
But only looked like a frog

Doing the Triangle Pose
Cannot even see my toes
Trying the Seated Forward Fold
Only feeling more than old

Doesn't seem like a younger age
Still look as if I am overweight
Is all this just madness?
Perhaps I need more practice

Doing a wall-assisted handstand
Forgot about my bad back
Rolling forward ever so slow
Then out the lower window

Possessed

Had a date with a girl whom I desired
Her beauty was everything I admired
We would meet at the fashionable disco
Where I danced like some weirdo

Patiently stood at the leather bar
In she came, looking like a hot star
Her clothes were draped like honey
The art on her lips dripped so sultry

Dancing as we greeted each other
My desire would never ever recover
At that moment, she suddenly stopped
Frozen in time, my love then coughed

Her big eyes turned from blue to red
Some strange bulges formed on her neck
Her head quickly thrust backwards
Then she called me a godless bastard

At this point, I knew something was wrong
She then spewed green slime at the next song
To be honest, I didn't fear what come next
At this point, she was already better than my ex

Can't Wait for the Day to End

Today, I am mixing with the public
Only a few minutes, and I have had enough
Hypnotized by info on the smart phone
And the shake of any girl's silicone

Instinctively, they just follow another
Even though they can't stand each other
Just can't wait for the day to end
Wish I should have stayed in bed

Standing in line for a coffee or two
Others are so close, I don't have room
They have all the time in the world
Not realizing most of us have to work

Some of the people begin idle chit-chat
Begin to feel I am one of the damned
Don't need to hear about gas and taxes
Too bad I forgot to bring my antacids

The barista suddenly seems to disappear
Looking around there also isn't a cashier
Thinking how to end as I am quite clever
But it looks like I will be trapped forever

When Karma Hit Amber

Men equated to only money
Didn't matter if they were chubby
Her comfort was all that mattered
Lives were only her to tear into tatters

Any rich man in our town
Would soon be her clown
Waiting for her as she shopped
Paying at any high-class restaurant

Criss-crossing her shapely legs
Never needed them for sex
Along with her doctor-crafted rack
Instantly, these men were trapped

Afterwards, the men are so bruised
They know what it is like to be used
Usually sitting naked and so alone
Waiting for her to text or to phone

While waiting for her next victim
The one would give that golden ring
A car suddenly shoots shite upon her
Just as a millionaire exits an Uber

Do I Really Have To Clean?

Decided enough was enough
Should really clean up my stuff
Who knows what I will find?
The way I live; it's like I'm blind

The kitchen table comes first
But the bathroom is probably worse
Should clean though where I eat
Something smells worse than my feet

Stacking all the plates and boxes
I come across something so soggy
Perhaps, it may be an old calzone
But, somehow, it also looks frozen

Have some canisters of disinfectant
Think I may have just sprayed breakfast
Should have hired some professionals
As I have always confused my chemicals

Whatever I do, my home looks filthy
Don't have the will to be clean and shiny
Just what is that growing on that wall
Wish there was someone I could call

Chocolate Croissant

Don't need a lady
Honestly, that's crazy
All I need is croissant
With chocolate on top

Lying next to hot coffee
Holding it while I dream
Waiting to be picked-up
In that French-style cup

Today's life is simply mad
Politicians making us sad
Needing a chance to escape
From that chaos they make

Tired of waiting on love
It's like waiting for a bus
All I need is a croissant
Simply warm but not hot

Difficult not to eat fast
No way could it ever last
Should really have another
There's no reason to suffer

Driving Jesus

Really needed some extra cash
Now an Uber driver, can't be that bad
Just got a call near the local church
Picked up a guy dressed as a Shepard

Quickly looked up the pick-up name
It read *Jesus*; must be some kind of game
Almost hit someone in the crosswalk
He muttered some words about God

Knew I shouldn't have drunk that
Now, my driving is under holy attack
Just said something about a sharp turn
Don't like his holier than thou concern

Have to get into the other lane
Shouldn't have waited to change
Holed hands grasping at the door
Sandals might go through the floor

Quickly U-turning to drop Jesus off
His mouth is seemingly about to froth
Turning, I say sorry to the Son of God
Underneath his breath, he says, "You Sod"

A Little Prick

Went to visit the family doctor
Berating me as if I was a sinner
Everything was wrong in my life
More annoying than my wife

Had to change my current lifestyle
Have to do things simply worthwhile
Daydreamed at the hanging skeleton
Thinking of the dangers of medicine

The doctor didn't look well at all
Unfit, bald, and his pants were too small
Should I be listening to this man's advice
Clearly, he was not living the best life

He told me that I should be vaccinated
The worst words I could have imagined
Telling him that I never, ever, get the flu
He took my words as if I were being rude

So, I sat in a waiting-to-be jabbed section
My name was soon called for injection
Hearing, "This shot will be a little prick."
Typical, as the doctor was a right…

His Tail

Thirst in quench
Down to my last cent
Entering a smokey café
A dead flower bouquet

A figure in tuxedo
Drinking a cappuccino
Slurps once or twice
Such noises are not nice

Sits in the seat next to me
No respect for my peace
A quick sip, he then slurps
Trying to say some words

His accent is slightly regal
Every syllable seems illegal
Speaking but breaking rules
As if he wants to be loose

Shifting a bit in his seat
Much to my disbelief
His tail wags and curls
Mocking me as it swirls

Gooey-Bubbling Froth

Always hated visiting my scientist relatives
After each visit, I needed to take sedatives
Observing my each and every move
If I tinkered with my fork or my spoon

Thought it would change when I got older
If anything, the critiques became bolder
How I sat even came under question
Always a comment about my pronunciation

Convinced their children were made from parts
Only knew rhetoric with unfeeling hearts
They played complex, mathematical games
Just to show us whom had the gifted brains

One day, they gave us a tour of the laboratory
Didn't look inviting but only just really gory
There were animals in formaldehyde
Bubbling solutions with a bobbling eye

Becoming tired, I put my drink on a machine
Didn't realize they like their equipment clean
As they screamed for me to take the glass off
Slipping, it exploded into a gooey-bubbling froth

Caught in Traffic

The day always ends in traffic
Modern life's worst demographic
Everyone just wants to drive home
But yet are distracted by an I-Phone

Always those going right
Waiting until the worst time
Then, those going left
Whose cars always have a dent

At the point where cars do not move
Changing lanes at this point turns rude
People just do not seem to understand
Decisions somehow go unplanned

Bored, I start playing with a button
Really, it must actually do something
Suddenly, the dashboard begins to beep
Should have paid more to get a Jeep

The driver over begins to stare at me
Smiling, she is awfully hairy and burly
Sitting still, I just get text after text
Frightfully, she wants to meet at the exit

Be So Hip You Hop

Modern life is full of men so square
Trimmed beards and cropped hair
It goes against nature to be clean
Being dirty makes a human being

Polka dot ties; a polka dot shirt
Be a style that just may hurt
Wear striped pants all vertigo
With each step; be a Romeo

I'm just so hip that I hop
The drum, a dance of song
My footsteps move the floor
Driving the beat ashore

Take off those baseball hats
Also don't be like aristocrats
Nature is never artificial
A man's gotta move his nipple

Don't be afraid to somersault
You may just land in a heart
Be so hip that you hop
Roll around until you are on top

Served

In a rush, with other places to be
Gotta trim the salt in my goatee
Must also post a package for a friend
Afraid of what I will have to spend

The line is long and is not moving
Workers are working, but deceiving
Their movements are only an illusion
Any kind of work is actually unproven

Waiting in this cold room is so painful
With all the employees so ungrateful
Before long, I become the next in line
But quickly told to wait by a held-up sign

I'm then told to go in another queue
My long wait begins yet anew
Stating that I am now in a rush
Still in line no matter what she does

The employing serving me disappears
Suddenly, a different employee appears
As I wait, another person slowly strolls in
She's quickly served; honestly, I just can't win

Black Bikini

If there is anything I have learned
Women have always ruled the world
Especially when wearing a black bikini
Everything else doesn't have meaning

The toughest man will become soft
A priest will stop being a man of the cloth
Doesn't matter if she is blonde or brunette
Any man alive with begin to sweat

This way will be always what will be
It's something both sexes would agree
A woman will never get a man's attention
If she doesn't look like she fell from Heaven

If there is anything I have learned
Men's dreams do not belong in a church
Especially when they are at the beach
With women covered with suntans and bleach

The roughest man will become a baby
A graying pensioner will think he is not aging
Doesn't matter if she is smart or well read
In a black bikini, any man will simply beg

Autocorrected

Jane was looking for love
Tired of one date a month
So, she tried online dating
All the men, just irritating

Didn't do well with a phone
Couldn't see the words shown
Would never wear her glasses
Never the subject of ballads

Meeting man after man
Wishes they never rang
All became obsessive
Losing all their senses

Men seemed to go mad
About where she shopped at
She abbreviated Trader Joe's
And no other words

When she seemingly texted
Her words were auto corrected
Somehow how typed T's
Became changed to B's

A New Swear Word

So many things wrong today
And the "all you can eat shite" buffet
Not enough swear words to use
Due to the lack of any truth

Swear words are just so common
The chorus and verse in life song
Doesn't one care about f____?
Freely spoken by the old and young

Not fazed by any profanity
Even professionals say them so clearly
But it does take a certain kind of a__
To graduate from any business class

Wasn't like this a few years ago
Life wasn't yet a total shite show
Women were yet to be called b____ces
Even in new age acoustic folk lyrics

Society needs a new swear word
Only the old ones are heard
Life, we know, needs a bit of kick
Tired of hearing the same ol' s____

I Love You (But Not You)

Desire walked in through the doors
For her beauty, there wasn't any words
Made my move and chatted her up
Looking into her eyes, I only felt love

Promising we would text each other
Instinct told me she would be my lover
Looking into her eyes one more time
Simply, her love would truly be mine

Sent the first text when I came home
It was hard not to call her on the phone
Playing hard to get, she didn't reply
In the morning, I texted one more time

Didn't hear a ping as the day went on
Just felt that something was wrong
Decided to heat things up a little bit
A more sensual, I really must admit

Sent text after text about making love
And that once could never be enough
Finally got a text after asking what went wrong
Sadly, I had been texting my co-worker, John

Dead or Alive

Bounty on my head
Due to my words said
Tore up conformity
Never will control me

High price to be paid
Stealing games they played
Taking all they ever gave
To tombstone and grave

Wanted dead or alive
But I'll never die
Too quick for their lies
To clever and wise

Following my trail
Never to any avail
Ignoring laws and rules
Burned fire and fumes

Wanted Dead or Alive
But I'll always survive
Can't kill me, ten lives
No matter hard one tries

You Really Gotta Hold On Me

Been on hold for what it seems like hours
My patience has long since been soured
Passed from voice to voicemail many times
Could communicate better with office mimes

Listening to music created by an office cretin
Couldn't stand it anymore, not even a second
Time is not one's friend when one is waiting
Their customers, it seems, they are evading

Suddenly, it feels as if I have to relief myself
Crossing my legs, to stop my bladder downstairs
They won't know if I am in the bathroom
Could be doing some work in my bedroom

The music stops, so I listen with a sharp ear
No fun waiting for an employee to answer
After a second, I hear yet another click
Suddenly, it goes back to that annoying music

Before long, my bladder bubbles with a sound
Inside, I feel like a volcano housebound
Running I relieve myself to a life paradigm
While my phone suddenly starts Facetime

How I Cam To Be

Heard all about the new craze
How singles spend their days
Posing nude using a web cam
Not really giving any damn

Lost my decades-old job
Friends consulted on my loss
One told me about web cams
Just be nude and use my hands

Very easy to set up my account
Could even accept British pounds
Women don't mind a bit of paunch
Surprised on the views on the launch

Became an overnight sensation
Just a few days, my fans went crazy
Only had to take a little bit of risks
To compensate for a bit of shrinkage

Soon, I will set up my OnlyFans
More money for my wiggle and dance
Pray I don't get erectile dysfunction
Because this cam is now my pension

You Might Be Beautiful (If I Could Only See You)

Been in love with her for years
Her face though never appears
She covers it with an accessory
But not single one is necessary

Don't know why, perhaps she's ugly
I don't know if she's even lovely
Perhaps, she may be quite pretty
In fact, all of this is quite a pity

To top it off, she wears sunglasses
The lenses are also just so massive
So, in a sense, one hardly sees her skin
Or If she Is pouting or has a lovely grin

She daily changes her mask or scarf
Some might think she may have a scar
I'm willing to bypass this little fault
As my heart aches whenever we are apart

Honestly, I haven't seen her face at all
Always covering herself with a shawl
Luckily, she does go to bed in the nude
So her coverings don't need to be removed

Gift from Above

Since a young boy, Albert wanted a garden
His vegetables would make him a fortune
Born with an eternal green thumb
Taught by his grandmother while young

Finally, he had a chance with a new home
The clouds opened and the lights shone
The apartment was on the ground floor
It had a garden, didn't care about the décor

The stories were as high as the blue sky
He planted as soon as he could occupy
Sadly, the area had a bit of drought
Praying, there came rain from above

Albert only could only ever smirk
His neighbors only ever had hard dirt
Every day, the rain came at the same time
He didn't question it or even ask why

At one point, he stood out in the rain
A neighbor yelled he must be insane
Albert still thought it was gift from God
But it was the emptying of a chamber pot

Risen to the Occasion

Middle age seemed to be creeping in
My wonderful tan became spots on skin
A friend recommended me a solution
Could be the next stage in evolution

All I had to do was take a pill a day
One by one, my decay would just go away
In the end, I would have youthful energy
Feeling as if I was born in this century

Before long, I began to win every race
No other runner could match my pace
In the gym, I could exercise for hours
Every muscle rose up to new powers

Women all over, turned their eyes
All to glance at my steel-made thighs
Their boyfriends also began to flirt
My legs are fit as any under a skirt

At a wedding, I danced and danced
Stole some kisses when I had a chance
Was able to catch the bride's garter
When a thought made me harden

Funkytown

Cleaning is for only squares
Don't have such reasonable cares
Don't believe about any disease
My reputation is built on sleaze

My trash goes out the window
To shower those passing below
Don't worry about whom I may hit
Probably deserves it - the little shit

Raised to be so eco unfriendly
My house could be labeled deadly
Authorities try very hard to condemn
But, in the end, I always do win

Black mold is the art on my walls
My underwear sometimes crawls
Bleach is a foul, six-letter word
Never have I ever cleaned any shirt

Plastic containers litter every room
I have fears of using my sole broom
Stench comes from clothes I wear
To be honest, I really just do not care

Leaf Blower

Satan comes in all forms
Doesn't always wear horns
May wear dirty baseball caps
With a leaf blower in his hands

Early morning, late at night
Satan enjoys working overtime
Gets paid with fear and anger
Just like a dirty city banker

His best weapon of choice
That leaf-blower of a big noise
Shape changing in the suburbs
Along cracked pavement and gutters

Blowing before sunrise one morning
Starting before giving any warning
Waking neighbors near and far
As obnoxious as a muscle car

He's also known to suck in souls
Doesn't care about skin nor bones
So, beware young fathers with a mower
True evil lies behind that leaf blower

Good Fortune

Wanted to impress a lady
So, she could be mine, maybe
I'm not just your average baboon
Saw she liked a certain perfume

Presented it to her one day
Along with a rose bouquet
She gave me a hug and a kiss
In return I admired her hips

Good Fortune was its name
Sparkly like good champagne
Little would she ever know
It's a replica; I'm a cheap Romeo

One drink led to five more
Then we stripped what we wore
Rolling around on the hotel bed
Didn't care if we fell on either head

Waking up, she's covered in fur
That cheap perfume reacted with her
Quickly dressed and called for a cage
Don't want to be around when she wakes

Loser Boyfriend

Hair gelled and styled
Dressed in pastels so vile
Symbol of the latest fashion
Mustache ends so waxen

He cannot pay any rent
Money already spent
Seduced by chiseled features
The sign of known cheaters

Disco was not just last year
No need to be a frilly mutineer
Who needs a dance floor?
Those neon lights only bore

How does it really feel?
Do date a boy with no appeal
Doesn't matter in the end
He's fashionable to a friend

Don't need a loser boyfriend
Who doesn't have money to lend
Date someone ugly and short
As at least, he, can fix the toilet

The King and The Queen

Behind the flash of a coat
In the shiny castle behind the moat
A king ruled with no rules
Surrounded by perfume and boobs

All the ladies tried to seduce him
With dyed hair and tanned skin
Never found his true princess
No matter how sexy her dress

Been this way for many years
Many women have shed tears
The wizard said it will soon be seen
The king will find his beloved queen

One day while annoying peasants
Came a beauty with such presence
Beautiful as the sun on a flower
She was sugar he could devour

Seducing her with gold and silver
There were fangs behind his whisker
Taking off her clothes that night
She was a he; the wizard was right

In the Sand

Thrown away by a beachgoer
I'm what everyone steps over
Come to ride the blowing storm
My art is what is performed

Many kids come to play with me
Usual tradition by the green sea
Carried by birds who are jealous
Dropped when they become restless

Everyone just wants to touch
But dropped when it's lunch
Never taken to a permanent home
Surprisingly popular but all alone

A young kid does try once in a while
The parents just lovingly smile
But, I'm always tossed as they leave
Knew it would come, I'm not naïve

Here comes a man now
Deep in speedo and a frown
But he quickly comes to smile
While he puts me in his mouth

Won't Grow A Mustache

Rebels don't follow fashion
They follow what they imagine
A mustache is such an example
Don't need that dirty handle

Grabbing crumbs is the only purpose
A pair of lips don't need curtains
Don't need to smell lunch all day
Who really needs a face toupee?

Men, these do not make you tough
Curled edges you look like a boy-puff
Hard-edge shaving makes a real man
A mustache looks like a boomerang

Have you thought what crawls around?
The creepy crawlers on your mouth
Should be enough to make you squeal
With them waiting for a small meal

So, I won't grow a mustache
Don't wanna be a wire-hair scumbag
A man's face should be smooth
Not a tussle of hair so crude

Sister Mary Screwed

Sister Mary finished screwing in the last nut
Adhering an electric pencil sharper was tough
Screwed it to the confessional box
Saving her a short but long walk

A woman enters wearing a low-cut top
Father Tom sweats in his confessional box
Her skirt rises as she kneels to pray
Signing a cross, God has just made his day

My dear, just tell me how long has it been?
Father, I can't tell you how much I've sinned
Start at the beginning and tell me everything
Father, my sins are sexual; you probably won't believe

Sister Mary goes to sharpen a worn pencil
Just when the lady begins the part so sensual
Irritated, the priest knocks on his confessional door
Missing out on other sexual acts she has performed

Suddenly, Sister Mary quits her pencil sharpening
The priest tries to distract by thinking of gardening
But as the lady talks about her affair with an anchorman
Sister Mary walks over to the sharpener once again

Exercising Demons

Been bored during the plague
This must have been a mistake
I make people scream and yell
Not a virus escaped from a vial

Got a letter from my manager
His ideas left me with only anger
Seems we demons must exercise
Our costumes are now an extra size

We are to meet for daily yoga
We'll never catch that corona
We demons can easily coexist
But this guidance is just so strict

Good to see my fellow demons
They will never vacation to beaches
All looking so pale and ghoulish white
Only wanting to give humans a fright

We are all just not that motivated
Some ghouls I think are intoxicated
Stretching now to try and get in shape
Looking sexier but still having inner hate

Island Man

Nothing matters but a perfect tan
Sun, movement, the island man
Painted birds stealing crystalline blue
Making feathers flowers in a tattoo

Silhouettes against the white sand
Sand, falling, the island man
Waves crashing into waves
Spelling out haunting names

Playing songs – dotting the breeze
Touching the inspiration overseas
Floating like a leaf, in the atmosphere
Falling as if a thrown spear

The island man picks up the leaves
Each one the color of lost dreams
Placing them in the shape of body
In a pose which never says I'm sorry

A storm brews on the horizon
Brought on by the call of a siren
A cast away washes up on the beach
Now, should he be cooked or steamed

Double-Triple Chocolate Cake

A woman doesn't need to flash cleavage
To turn any room from cold to heated
She only has to flash a BLT sandwich
To many any man feel as if on catnip

Men are suckers for any kind of food
Really a woman doesn't have to be nude
They instantly fall head over heals
For scrumptiously cooked meals

If a woman really wants a good man
She doesn't have to lie for a perfect tan
All she has to do is bake a good cake
Doesn't have to bother with a steak

Traditional love doesn't matter to a man
His love comes hot served from a pan
Ladies, double your triple chocolate cake
Its quality will equate to what he will take

Spread your icing thick as thick can be
With the thickness, any man will never disagree
To seal the deal, have some residue on your lips
So when he is finished, you'll also be delicious

The Monk

Tired of constantly thinking about sex
Frustrated by all the nudes sent by text
Picked up a pamphlet about being a monk
Initially, thought it was a bunch of junk

Being free of the phones and the internet
Well, just sat there and endlessly wept
Could now tell people my own name
No longer would I hang my head in shame

Didn't need any formal kind of education
Just be able to quickly learn meditation
A good voice doesn't matter for chants
Only singing about Saints from France

One day, female maids arrived with low tops
Suddenly, my soul began to melt, I got the hots
The sun said they needed to have some diversity
But, what will happen with all the women around me

After awhile, we chatted and began to hug
Overtime, with each maid, started to fall in love
But, being in a convent, it must be a sign from God
So, how could any lust really be wrong?

Sleaze Hippies

Please do not sit next to me
Don't need to hear your tragedy
Have enough problems in my life
No need to hear how we will all die

The world is not really dying
Please stop all your rebel trying
Complaints are falling on deaf ears
Just irritating after all these years

The world won't end if you wash
Sleaze hippies just please stop
Life as you know will continue
Not everything needs an issue

Only mixing fury with laziness
The ying to the yang of atheists
The man can sometimes be good
Like religion, he is misunderstood

Sandals are so out of fashion
Not a crime to live in a mansion
Wishing for you to fit into society
But, we know, you won't go quietly

X-Rayed

No one cleaned during the pandemic
Such was the case at my X-ray clinic
Despite everyone's worry and concern
Everyone was also at their worst

Many vermin slowly crept in
Everything began to look so grim
Even spiders arrived to feast
But one became a radioactive beast

Upon a bite, one began to change
My bite felt good despite the pain
Strangely, I began to see through clothes
Had a new super-power I suppose

From a parrot tattoo on a man's tit
To a lady's legs with waves and a ship
A burly ape on a woman's buttock
To a sock tattooed under a sock

Was truly enjoying this new gift
Until a Whole Lotta Susie walked in
Saw a tattoo just above her tootsie
A Chippendale that looks just like me

Better Be Annoying (Before Annoying Annoys You)

There are a few things I learned in life
One doesn't get ahead while being nice
To get ahead, one must be more than ruthless
Be a boil on the bum, an utter nuisance

If you are waiting in life, just nag others in line
Before long, they will depart in a matter of time
Suddenly, you will be the next one to be served
It's good to be the leader, and not the herd

In a relationship, be the first one to nag
You will never be the one who becomes mad
Your calmness will ensure your point of view
It's so genius, the others won't know the coup

While driving about in any crowded city or town
One will come across a driver who is a clown
Before the driver attempts to enter your lane
Blow your horn, so the car never does change

Eating out can be a royal pain in anyone's ass
Be annoying to staff, before they have the chance
If one complains to the manager more than once
You will be better served the next time you come

Art Class

Couldn't believe I ran out of bob
So, I began to look for an extra job
Always looked after myself
Regarded me simply top shelf

Found an ad for nude model
I'll do it if it isn't unlawful
Sent in my photos and resume
Got the job, as if they couldn't wait

Headed down to the local college
Quite proud of my good package
The teacher greeted me with a smile
And told me to put my clothes in a pile

Nervous, entering, I stood and posed
Forgetting where I was without any clothes
The class looked a little bit bemused
Perhaps, they liked how I groomed

Before I knew it, class was over
Some complained about my exposure
Apparently, this wasn't an art class
But one of a rather complicated math

Shrink, Shrank, Shrunk

God gifted me when I was born
My manhood was made for porn
Ladies would sway and swoon
At what my pants would balloon

Blessed with many wild nights
Spent with angels of earthly delights
Some say the nights were only titillation
But, for most, my love was an education

Over the years, I began to notice
My manhood was smaller in togas
What used to bounce so freely
Couldn't come to do a wheelie

Didn't think too much about it
As it would work with a strip
But the balloon would soon deflate
Becoming my normal trait

Now, my passion lies elsewhere
Not with a lovely derrière
But with an early fruit brunch
As I shrink, shrank, and shrunk

Don't Care If I Ever Deliver

Come rain, snow, or sleet
Too tired on my two feet
Carrying bills and junk mail
Adverts with TVs on sale

Don't care if I ever deliver
My mail pouch also has liquor
Keeps me warm in my truck
Heat only works with luck

Barking dogs are just not cute
The way they nip at my boot
Nothing cute about being bit
Somedays, I could just quit

There are also the gossip queens
Never straying from there themes
Telling me about the recent affair
Now, as if I really did ever care

Don't care if I ever deliver
On the job, I am not a drinker
Happily drunk to my favorite song
While dropping mail on your lawn

So What?

Beauty dripping blonde
A lyre to my song
Red lips in sexy puck
Breasts; that perfect tuck

Many men desire
Hearts burn on fire
She just can't be real
Eyelash paint appeal

Svelte gorgeousness
Just want what is next
Her smile is so veneer
Seductive; the white sneer

Many men ache
From women so fake
Never ever wanted your love
Dudes are just so dumb

So what with beauty!
Rather have a cutie
One who can just boogie
Not just show off her booty

That Sinking Feeling

Old-Leather hands toss me
Into the deep blue sea
Shifting, I slowly sink
Then I begin to think

What did I do to deserve this?
When did the Captain's jealousy begin?
Did I seduce his favorite concubine?
She did tell me she was only mine

Saved the crew without a compass
Navigated stars when the sun set
Escaped natives so unfriendly
While the crew drank to a sea-shanty

Did I steal a gold coin or two?
During that pillage at Cancun
Thought no-one would notice
When storing the boxes in the hold

Blue fades from my view as I sink
Shouldn't have done what I did
Wiggling free my legs and wrists
I, though, must stop taking these risks

Don't Want to Fly Today

The alarm rings at the time set
This noise I must condemn
Don't want to wake up
Tired of flying, just had enough

Always the same crowd
Travelers shouting so loud
The attendants don't care
Shouldn't really be in the air

Airport traffic just bites
People are parasites
Rushing to here and there
Too close before they appear

Americans are just the worst
Always a rude word and t-shirt
Never anything about beauty
Always about booty or a booby

Waiting in the lounge is torture
Balls of stress waiting for departure
Might be just a little bit biased
As it is my first week as a pilot

So What?

Beauty dripping blonde
A lyre to my song
Red lips in sexy puck
Breasts; that perfect tuck

Many men desire
Hearts burn on fire
She just can't be real
Eyelash paint appeal

Svelte gorgeousness
Just want what is next
Her smile is so veneer
Seductive; the white sneer

Many men ache
From women so fake
Never ever wanted your love
Dudes are just so dumb

So what with beauty!
Rather have a cutie
One who can just boogie
Not just show off her booty

Where's the Check

Henry's hearing is not so good
Everything gets misunderstood
Cannot understand life anymore
Always hearing that annoying roar

He had a date at a restaurant
With that one classless blonde
The one who has dated everyone
No matter how smart or dumb

The meal was going rather well
Felt that they would end up in a hotel
She nibbled on his right earlobe
Left lipstick like Dracula on his throat

Lost in thought of lust and passion
Didn't see the waiter choking by his table
Asking the waiter on the floor for the check
Not seeing that he would soon be dead

Oblivious to the frantic situation
Thinking it was different implication
Regretting he didn't act any sooner
As he knows the Heimlich maneuver

A Hat Trick

George decided to learn some magic
So he could swoon women with a trick
Nothing else had ever seem to work
Tired of a woman's uninterested smirk

The best magic books were written in Latin
The words he didn't understand -- he imagined
Once in a while, there was a puff of smoke
Sometimes, a lady became a bearded bloke

Before he knew it, a girl caught his eye
The type that you never want to hear a goodbye
Not dismayed, he continued on despite fear
If all failed, he would magically disappear

His performance brought a rave review
People came for his sexy, and dark, voodoo
To win her heart, he researched a hat trick
It had to be big, and so worth the risk

Waving a wand over the hat, he said a Latin word
He was so excited that her words he had misheard
Storming out of the club, she called him a sicko
As the surprise in the hat was a penis pillow

Coffee and a Cigarette

A few days since he had been crucified
Tales were told he would rise after some time
Decided to see for myself down at the crypt
Never know, it might be some kind of trick

A huge stone blocked his burial place
To move it would be a matter of faith
Old ladies knelt and endlessly cried
Chuckled to myself if it was all just a lie

Vendors were already there selling souvenirs
Jesus on the cross, with multiple mirrors
Rumor, he approved them while at the last meal
Prices so low, one might think it was a steal

People were getting shifty, antsy and nervous
We shouldn't have listened to a guy shirtless
One day turned into two and soon will be three
This story was becoming too hard to believe

Suddenly, the sky crashed with thunder and light
The stone in front moved with a strong natural might
Jesus exited wiping his eyes while all around wept
Then said, "Does anyone have coffee and a cigarette?"

First Impressions

Destined to go to hell
Despite coins in the wishing well
Heaven never really appealed
As such, my fate was sealed

Asked to pay the ferryman
No coins in either hand
Gave him a smart-ass remark
Seems he doesn't want to talk

Have an appointment with Satan
Hope he is at least shaven
I appreciate a first impression
Leads to a deeper connection

Rejected yesterday at Heaven
Perhaps, it was something I said
Saints looked a bit disappointed
So, my application was voided

Waiting in a velvet-red room
Assistant said he will be there soon
Hoping for the right words
Don't need those pitchfork burns

Rock N' Roll Blues

Oh Chuck, debauchery is still in my song
But somehow Rock N' Roll has gone wrong
Throwing TV's out the window isn't the same
The smash isn't right with a thin frame

Can't drink Jack Daniels anymore like water
Even a few glasses I run to the doctor
My day was getting high then playing on stage
Now, I prefer vegetarian meals backstage

What happened to that hell-bent rebellion?
Now, only waiting when will I get indigestion
Used to have models on every other arm
Now, I'm lucky if any lady is warm

Oh Jerry, I used to jump when in music halls
Can't do as such as my prostrate is enlarged
Remember baths filled with imported champagne
My bath clogs now due to the hair in the drain

Drugs littered the floor of my hotel room
My pallor was if I just stepped out of a tomb
These days, my room is filled with vitamin pills
As at moment, I may get some chills

When I Was Rowdy

Soaking in a soapy, steamy bath
Remember when I used to be bad
For me to wash was a miracle
Yet my dirty self was so kissable

To destroy was my way of life
Now I think I should have a wife
Perhaps, I'm growing tired of drink
Desire only to scrub and clean the sink

Oh, the times when I was rowdy
Where I roamed just so free
Now, I have to be close to a lavatory
As my stomach now is a laboratory

Parties happened when I walked in
I wrote the Ten Commandments of sin
Just can't be bothered with others
Only want to be with my cat under covers

My cologne was cigarettes and whiskey
My fashion was entirely so filthy
Have only the desire to shower and shave
Just what is it with this desire to behave?

Rock N' Roll Prescription

Been feeling kinda normal
My behavior now is moral
Feeling sick, must see the doctor
But. I'm down to my last dollar

Heavy metal music in the lobby
Everything seems just so naughty
Nurses with only a garter and a belt
Guitars cover up any patient's yell

Rock N' Roll is what I need
Just a taste of the peach
Is all I need for good health
Then I will feel like myself

My doctor enters the room
Probes all deep into my gloom
Saying he is just what I need
Better than aspirin and sleep

Scribbling on a piece of paper
Telling me to fill it now not later
The prescription reads Rock N' Roll
Thus allowing me to lose control

Fountain of Youth

Found the elixir of youth
Bought from the queen of truth
Drinking, my skin became smooth
My clothes were once again loose

Soon as I walked through the door
Many ladies were there to adore
With my youth, I'd surely score
In fact, I'm too hard to ignore

Chatting to a beauty before long
Our hearts beat rather strong
As she sung her favorite song
Well, I knew something was wrong

Could never ever be with her
Her tastes are not what I prefer
Wishing things what they were
And just what did I do this for

The Queen didn't have another elixir
Nor did she have another mixture
My life is now to be lived on tinder
Swiping ladies who look like a stripper

Nothing Wrong with Cheating

As I sit in my jacuzzi with a sexy lady
Amazed at my success as I am so lazy
Never received an A or a good grade
Spent most of my time in the arcade

People ask how I have achieved in life
Simple, all I have done is just lie
No reason to put effort into anything
No reason to be in pain at the gym

In the end does it really matter
How one climbs the social ladder
As long as one makes it to the top
Doesn't matter if its right or wrong

Seen my share of bastards who studied
Acting so arrogant with their money
Treating people as if they are peasants
Just because they had an inheritance

Nothing wrong with my behavior
I've won on a simple life wager
Nothing wrong with achieving
By only doing a little bit of cheating

Never Going to Catch me

Smoke from my gun
The deal is done
The price was met
My bargain was kept

Contract signed
With the devil's lies
Life is ink and paper
Death then comes later

Never going to catch me
Never going to find me
Justice founded on a lie
Never will I ever die

The law is unjust
Liberty is blindfolded
Hands behind her back
Evil lipstick in her laugh

Never going to catch me
Laws will never find me
One day I'll be the devil
And your soul I will sell

Yet Another Way to Die

Again, Destiny laid out her cards
Just like love I refused her arms
Met a lady who was long and lean
To many men, she was the queen

Men paid to keep her beauty
Her looks so blonde and moody
When the money seemed to run out
A man's heart would soon be plowed

Some men thought they could sin
Only then did their problems begin
No man could seem to keep up
She would turn them into dust

One day, we met under a full moon
Not realizing it would lead to my tomb
Before long, she took all she could
No questions; always understood

One day, my credit card became overdrawn
Every single account of mine – withdrawn
Only then did I notice the chloroform rags
And the scattered vials of anthrax

Handheld Device

Went to see the local theatre
Only free seats were in the center
Saying sorry; moving as I leaned
Finally found one that was free

The lady next to me was full of hate
No way she could have been on a date
Remembered I didn't have confectionary
Leaving, the people didn't have sympathy

Returning, they all had to stand up again
As I sat, there was a stare from that woman
The lights dimmed and people opened snacks
Somehow, in excitement, I dropped my packs

Everything was lost even the candy and popcorn
My phone suddenly activated and went wrong
Mistakenly, I had it in my front pants pocket
Swear I had left it behind in the car docket

Sitting back, I thought how could this be?
Can't watch any movie without a Jujube
Suddenly, everyone looked at me with scorn
Seems like I accidentally activated my porn

Nothing is Beautiful Before 10:00 a.m.

Putting on eyelashes and make-up
Her beauty turns a bit more animated
No use going out early in the morning
The only men out are the ones balding

Sitting naked, admiring her tanned body
Her every inch has become glossy
Doesn't have to think she is a top model
Even her little mole is a sparkle

Let the other girls in the town jog about
They have their reasons due to a pouch
By God's design, no need to exercise
Jealous, she is the reason why the devil lies

Dressed in white and decorative lace
Her fashion is the epitome of a babe
Women define the tone of jealousy
After only one look, most need therapy

Gathering her items to venture outside
Yoga-Women immediately become terrified
Their sexy pants just cannot even compare
Nothing comes close to her derrière

Morally Condomed

Billy played women like the lottery
Every girl seemed to step out of a dream
At the age of 40, he acted like a teenager
Didn't care if he slept with any stranger

One day, his sister, Anne, asked him for a favor
Well, she should have asked another Sailor
Her little boy, Tommy, needed to be watched
She had to do a procedure down at the doc

Being the softy he is, he said he would
Thinking about it she wondered if he should
But, in reality, there wasn't anyone else
He agreed as she need to have good health

It started off fine, but they went to the pub
One drink let to another, never enough
Chatting up with one lady after another
He eventually found one to be his lover

Back at the flat, passion let to make love
Tommy, in another room, found a cupboard
Finding condoms, he blew them up to pass time
All, but one, were floating, much to Billy's surprise
Just what is it with this desire to behave?

Just Can't Suck Today

So tired today and so not motivated
My body just isn't blood caffeinated
Can't get out of this closed coffin
All day, I've been standing and tossing

My victims are not healthy anymore
All have become an annoying herbivore
Men are weak, nothing to tuck into
Horrible taste with a lady's tattoo

I'm withering like a rose on a vine
To survive is not committing a crime
All I want to do is just suck
But everyone is a healthy schmuck

Born from evil, I'm a child of the devil
But for that please don't be judgmental
Tempted to hunt in the late afternoon
Surely, I can hide in a nearby tomb

Perhaps, I should drink with another vampire
Or find a virgin, or something, for even that matter
But, today, I can't be bothered to suck
Tired of humans – I've just had enough

Frankly Dear, You Can Just Kiss It

Don't need somebody to criticize
Or someone to bring me down to size
So, frankly dear, you can just kiss it
My ties will always be ones that clip

Should be able to wear a sombrero
With my fancy dress, rhinestone tuxedo
To dance the night away is my right
Need another lady who has less appetite

Don't need somebody to complain
Or someone to tell me I need a brain
So, frankly dear, you can just kiss it
My desserts will always have Cool-Whip

Should be able to wear those tiny shorts
You know I always wear good supports
No need to worry about a manhood surprise
My grapes always stick close to the vines

Don't need somebody to condemn
Or a woman who tries to change men
So, frankly dear, you can just kiss it
Tired of humans – I've just had enough

Bandits

Bullet straps strung along their backs
Stealing from those who wear slacks
Unshaven and mustaches grown too long
Stepping on spring flowers along the lawn

Bandits have again ridden into town
Crusty older men who wear a frown
All seem to have lost their edge
Underwear slanted on the wedge

Lost their bullets years ago
Their songs once played on the radio
To them, the internet doesn't make sense
Staring at screens is only a pretense

What used to be arms of shining metal
Are now wobbly arms of a worn-out rebel
No reason now to keep oneself in shape
Life is no longer judged by one's age

Blowing kisses at all the young ladies
Passion is only something for daydreams
But, if a lady would join and take a chance
Any bandit would only put out his bad back

So Dirty

No need to shave my legs
Men don't care if there is sex
If they have their wanton desire
Men don't care about a woman's attire

Haven't worn make up in a year
My wrinkles are as they appear
Men don't care as I am braless
Perky breasts are always a success

Doughnut stains on my t-shirt
Also the ones from yesterday's desert
Just cannot eat like a normal woman
Never a saint, nor am I from Heaven

As dirty as dirty could ever be
Some men consider this artsy
Don't need to take care anymore
Nothing is clean in any clothes drawer

No need to paint my nails
Doesn't matter to any of the males
My armpit hair is a sign of power
So, please don't ask for me to shower

Don't Mess With Texting

Cell phones will never be my thing
Never answered a single phone ring
My wife was mad she couldn't reach me
Wanted to take away my only dream

Never liked the idea of sending any text
In this marriage, I don't even want sex
Upon a flurry of a few sent messages
Always upset with my brief answers

Sitting there I found the on/off button
Would only tell of a service interruption
Clever in the art of smart phones
When I came home, I still got groans

Don't understand any emoji symbol
I always choose one that's not civil
Little did I know about the eggplant
Sending it to her friend was a deathtrap

For some reason, she took offense
It's her fault; as I really shouldn't text
Perhaps, I should also put on my glasses
Life is not worth these small chances

She's Crazy for You

Little did I know my cute smile
Would bring such a crocodile
Drinking with my mates at the pub
Had too many pints; had such a buzz

In the corner, sat a sexy concubine
Taunted as if her cleavage would be mine
Making my way over to the empty seat
I was just the next piece of meat

After our sordid one-night affair
Couldn't get her out of my hair
Suddenly, she was everywhere I turned
This fact had me, frankly, disturbed

Singing songs to me as I woke
Thought it was just a joke
There she was standing outside
From my window, I stood terrified

Chatted one day with my mate
Told him we didn't even have a date
He said that it is certainly taboo
But she is only crazy just for you

Don't Say I'm Beautiful – You Bastard

Spent over three hours preparing myself
All kinds of scattered make-up on the shelf
Turning the beautiful me into a pure Goddess
More than a model, more than girl gorgeous

When I walk down any busy city street
Men only come to trip over their own feet
Turning heads to look at my wonderful being
Amazed and can't believe what they are seeing

Once in a while some of them say I'm beautiful
They are all beneath me and just so delusional
Never, will they run their fingers through my hair
The fact is that I will only let them stand and stare

Now, don't say I'm beautiful you poor bastard
I'm not impressed by this nor am I flattered
Can't you see that I'm looking for one certain type
If you aren't a millionaire, don't even try

Now, don't say I'm the woman of your dreams
You will never ever find me between the sheets
Men, t think I am just nothing but a pure bitch
But my attitude will change if I find out you are rich

Opposites Don't Attract

Falling in love is a matter of hearts
Sometimes, it is written in the stars
It is also said that opposites attract
I've never seen this, so it just isn't fact

Don't see cheerleaders with gardeners
Don't see felons dating judges or wardens
It's just the way life isn't supposed to be
Birds have never dated the proverbial bee

Falling in love only means a broken heart
So, no need to wish upon any falling star
The wish will never ever seem to come true
Cupid is small, so he will always be cruel

Don't ever see businessmen dating cleaners
Don't see trophy wives going for dreamers
Destiny only works its way towards death
With love, it's only a slow game of chess

Falling in love can break any lover's heart
Usually, it burns out like a dying star
So, when people say opposites attract
Think first, as it will only be a trap

Fingered

Every workplace is horrific
The devil's only true gimmick
Doesn't help that my boss stinks
Every minute full of her politics

She always pulls my trigger
Likes to give me the finger
Licking it when turning a page
Or tearing off a piece of tape

Never does it directly towards me
But does it when others can't see
Leaving me with a bad feeling
Really do not know her meaning

Debating if I should return the finger
But she may poison my dinner
Lying in bed thinking of such things
Or if I washed the clothes with rinse

Waking up, I decided I would do it
She always thought I was a little shit
Gave her a gesture quite inspired
Turning to me, she said, "You're fired"

Dog Gone It

Why should I really care about anything?
Around here, I'm known to be the king
My existence is to be fed and to go poo
Give my slippers; I need something to chew

Everyone loves my fluffiness and cute ears
Don't mind if I eat until something disappears
Didn't care I ate that priceless table leg
Or the Persian Rug I can't help but to wet

They say an owner tends to look like the dog
In case of this family, this fact isn't wrong
My owner is a drop-dead slab of gorgeousness
Not unlike me, she loves to get well-dressed

One day, she sat me down to tell me something
Important but I acted as if it were nothing
Telling me a man came into her life
And would be visiting late that night

Immediately disliked him as he entered the door
Such a lounge-lizard attitude in what he wore
Never really adored or petted me, so I had enough
Stole his wallet, went to the toilet, then flushed

The Make-Up Artist

We met; it felt like lightening
Her painted fangs were so tempting
Just had to meet this lady of art
Whose arms bore her heart

Dated after a short while
Amazed from stars on her smile
Would never reveal her true face
Saying, "in the right time and place"

She could look like a mummy
Or a model so yummy
Never knew when she was tired
As her beauty was all I admired

Everyone thought she was so cute
With her hair dangling with fruit
My friends were just so jealous
She was cool, calm and rebellious

One day, she told me I was in for a surprise
For once, make-up free not telling more lies
I then thought I would lose my mind
She looked like the Bride of Frankenstein

Adam Was Eve'd

Living in the Garden of Eden
The never-ending perfect season
God created Adam and Eve
Love was all they could need

Near the crystal, blue stream
The devil appeared with his greed
Eve was wandering all by herself
Nature was all one needed for wealth

Stopping her, he offered a credit card
The kind with such a great reward
Informing her she could get anything
Despite she already had everything

Soon, Eve was addicted to shopping
With the intent of her never stopping
Adam didn't realize what was going on
Never shopped on the website Amazon

Didn't question the boxes at the oasis
Nor the new gold and silver bracelets
Only realized when he received a huge bill
Did Adam see Eve was seduced by the devil

Poison Ivy

Making her way into a sunset
Light caressing her neck
Upon shadowed cobblestone
Poison Ivy grows along the road

Moving as she walks by
Coming to life – that poison vine
A sole branch follows her
The town's little known saboteur

Stopping to read a message
The vine jumps at that second
Wrapping around her shoe
Adhesive oils just like glue

Rising upwards on her left leg
Higher with each soft step
Ringing around her torso
Decorating her pattern poncho

Doesn't seem to ever notice
She's turning into a poison lotus
Shocked when its covering her body
But then delighted as it looks so lovely

Paranotnormal

My panties disappear every night
Something is wrong and not right
Doesn't matter if they are frilly or lace
They disappear all just the same

Some say I have a poltergeist
Honestly, it's only looking for a heist
Who steals a lady's undergarment?
These can be bought at any market

The thefts leave me feeling flattered
Long time since I have even mattered
The thief isn't afraid of my girth and width
Just wonder who my admirer is?

Some say a ghost roams my house
Pitter-pattering without a sound
Always buy my panties in stock
No ghoul knows where they are bought

Wonder if it shares them with friends
And they talk about my lovely scents
Should tell them that I was once a man
But I'm the kind who likes an upper hand

Dracula Is My Mailman

Due to the lack of any good virgin
Dracula had to do job searching
Didn't care to get qualified
His resume was full of lies

No-one believed his resume
His skills were not for today
Dracula really tried to diversify
But old degrees didn't qualify

Must find some new kind of job
Had to sell his castle due to loss
Became a postman as a last resort
Couldn't face both daylight and court

Mail always has a bit of dried blood
In the end, who wants to touch?
May have bills in the thousands
But don't want disease on my hands

Never delivers mail before midnight
Some say they fear he may bite
Don't mind this touch of gothic
As my meals are made with garlic

The Influencer

Arriving from Paris unkempt
Showing sides of her breast
Paparazzi watching every move
So many young men to choose

All young ladies want to be her
Her parties are just a blur
She embraces nakedness
Hardly wearing any dress

Her heels stab catwalks
For her, rock stars sing songs
Not unlike a flash of lights
Desire, is what blinds

Spending an hour in NYC
Then she is back to Pari
Automatic pilot of a dream
A quick dash in a limousine

A selfie upon entering
No need for censoring
She only has to giggle
Then show a little nipple

Folk-Singer Son-In-Law

A daughter's husband is always a nightmare
Some are cool; some are still in a highchair
My daughter said she was getting married
Honestly, I just wanted to be only buried

Much to my horror, he was a folk singer
I'd rather she would run off with a drifter
Who really needs an acoustic balladeer?
Thank God I haven't given up dark beer

Over time, he started to sing at holidays
Hoping to find a seasonal gig that pays
Don't need to hear rehearsals at Christmas
Or Valentine Day's songs, which are worse

Could have married that Quarterback
But now I have become insomniac
Awake, listening to strums and a yelp
Where is Motorhead instead of this hell?

She could have married that bank manager
But now I listen to songs for a grandmother
They say kids always payback their parents
But, if this is the case, I'll spend the inheritance!

Nanasty

Being nice isn't cool anymore
Manners are something to ignore
My goal in life is to be Nanasty
I'm the one who calls you fatty

To criticize is how I live my life
Not my issue you have fatty thighs
Seemingly can't control yourself
Donuts are not visionary health

Don't like those who cut in line
Honestly, it is not really fine
Do this action to someone else
Do not speak to me as if I am twelve

Helping others just isn't cool either
Not into being an over achiever
Believe in an eye for an eye
No qualms about eating your pie

Tired of those who want to help
Take back your emails via unsend
Life is only really bitter-sweet
And bitter is what I want to keep

A Form of Expression

Jimmy wanted everything fast
Answers before they are asked
Wearing out impatience at birth
Aging, well, it only became worse

His energy was a spinning atom
Quickly revolving like an album
Faster and faster within a groove
Burning to the end of his fuse

His friends told him to relax
It's okay for him to just laugh
But, Jimmy didn't want to hear
Never knew how one should feel

Tasked to finish a hard project
His assistant was a blockhead
Always choosing a bad decision
One day, only to end up in prison

Their presentation was later that day
A disaster much to Jimmy's dismay
Prone to spontaneously combust
Exploding, leaving behind red dust

The Trash That Wouldn't Leave

They came from the Deep South
Where every town is a small town
Ripped, small t-shirts and overalls
Stained by sleeping in animal stalls

How could they be related to us?
Choosing your friends and not family sucks
We should really check out the full story
But Lord Simpson was just so naughty

Didn't matter if his lust was royalty
The only matter was a woman's buoyancy
Supposedly, these were some of his brood
Now, they are here eating all of our food

What will it take for them to leave us?
They have been here now for months
Even filthy when the Queen visits
Blowing kisses, her highness only grimaces

We have consulted voodoo witches
Even sacrificed some loved chickens
Sadly, it seems they will never leave
And now, they are naked at our soirée

Saw Mommy Stripping for Santa Claus

Tossing and turning on Christmas Eve
Many presents were in my dream
Loud noises awake me upon the roof
One reindeer endlessly taps her hoof

Hiding behind the tree, I look around
Soot, clouds, and laughs comes to sound
Looking at the cookies and milk laid out
Santa cheers and shouts a bit too loud

Holding his belly while it is shaking
My mother comes in almost naked
Dropping his cookies on the floor
Ms. Santa never had what she wore

Tempted, mommy did a little shake
Buns oiled as if they were ready to bake
Running her fingertips over stockings
Santa's cookies could only become soggy

Turning around, mommy took off her bra
Santa's glasses fogged from what he saw
Mommy said, "It's cold, do you really have go?"
Stopping, Santa then said, "Well, Ho, Ho, Ho."

Unsubscribed

Tired of the so-called modern life
Nothing about it is ever right
Just feel like life is nothing but a lie
Pressed my button and unsubscribed

Used to find my way without a phone
Now only sit in a crowded place all alone
Watching everyone wasting precious time
Want to press my button and unsubscribe

Feeling freedom, feeling thought
Realizing these were almost lost
Seeing color stolen by society
All for stacks of that green money

Swerving on a crowded sidewalk
Dazed people lost in cellphone talk
Not caring if the old life is gone
More important to shop on Amazon

Social media, the paint in confusion
That false freedom with its illusion
Only worth anything if any story is liked
Want to press my button and unsubscribe

History of the Poet's Collections

Being born with a poet's soul works against one in this modern age. This age doesn't warrant thought. It only wants followers and likes. Humanity has been trapped by greed and looks for thousands of years. To try and stop this evolution is valiant, but humanity has progressed too far down a path where it cannot recover. This modern age only wants a quick answers and fixes for questions. It doesn't want evolution. As a result, a thoughtful, progressive mind is met with confusion, dislike and downright loathing.

This history is just a taster for what the poet has gone through during his life. The poet began to write in the late 1980s. His first collection is entitled *Into the Forest* and was written in London, Dublin, and Warsaw during the early and mid 1990s. With youth on his side, the poet wandered through the streets of the various cities and detailed the innocence of life slowly being drained away from the world. Easily corrupted by power and money, the landscape of Europe was transforming to what currently exists now, a bastion of confusion, the lack of identity, and just plain dissatisfaction.

Jungle Blue, his second poetry collection began a fruitful writing period, but all of the poems are related as they hit on the theme of religion, fear, death, and the occasional brilliance of beauty. These were written upon the poet's return to the United States in 1999 and living in the Washington, D.C. area. Recent poems were added to this collection, about twenty-five poems were in the original publication in 2012, but a further thirty-five are recent aural poems. The remaining are extreme rewrites of poetry written in the same time period of *Into the Forest.*

The third poetry collection, *Vox Vibrato,* was written in the attempt to have comical poetry printed in daily newspapers every day. These poems were written mainly from 2003 to 2007. Since printed newspapers were dying, the editors and publishers were not so highly keen to entertain this material. This fact again reflects the state of the country where money, or the lack of it, has influenced art and why art is failing today.

Shadow Exotica, the fourth collection, was written in the 2008 to 2010 period. More accomplished and wanting to feel the aural affect that might have been missed on the earlier poems, the author wrote are what he feels is some of his best work. These poems grasp at the beauty of relationships, the grace of the wonders in this world, and the complexities of myths.

The fifth collection, *Read Without Caution,* was written in 2018 and 2019 as the poet finally felt free to write some prose after lengthy health, personal, and work difficulties, leaving him to where survivability was the only work. Embraced with the freedom and creativity returning, the work is some of the finest to date he has achieved.

No Read Limit, the sixth collection, deals with the New World due to the Pandemic. What was reality does not exist anymore. Loss of freedom, being trapped in a cellphone world, and disregard for others has taken its place. Compassion for others has been replaced for the quest of likes on a social-media platform. The seriousness of everyday tasks or functions has taken its toll as humor has been replaced. Everything must have reason, a money-exchange, and footprint in the digital world. The poems mock this modern world and what humanity has become. Freedom is naturally given, and it is on the precipice of being lost. How much are humans willing to give to be controlled by others? The collection depicts the little pieces of life where society is losing it bit by bit. The characters portray the followers, the conformists, and the fashionistas for what they are — tools of the failed political system. This collection was written from 2020 to early 2023.

www.ingramcontent.com/pod-product-compliance
Lightning Source LLC
Chambersburg PA
CBHW061731040426
42453CB00026B/649